The Broo
Would

Alex Hay

Illustrated by Kate Simpson

This is the story of how my brother
Pete made friends with a witch.

One day, when I was about seven,
I was walking along the road that
passed by the back of our house,
when I came across an old woman.

She looked a bit like a witch out of
one of the old fairy stories. She was
dressed nearly all in black, but her hat
was a round, fluffy mauve thing. It
was more like an old tea cosy. In her
hands she was holding a broomstick.

3

She was saying something to the
broomstick, and every now and again
she shook it. Then she picked it up
and bashed it on the ground.

"Is something wrong?" I asked.

"Wrong? Wrong? I'll say so!"

The old woman turned round as quick as a spinning top. She stood with her hands on her hips, while the broomstick remained upright behind her, swaying slightly.

"It's packed up on me." Her voice was creaky but strong, and she spoke quickly. "Stopped! Won't work!"

The old woman spun round again and gave the broom a walloping great kick.

The broom did a cartwheel and fell into the road on its side. It made a "pff" noise, and jerked a couple of times as though it was trying to get up. Then it lay still.

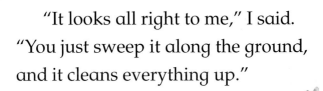

"It looks all right to me," I said. "You just sweep it along the ground, and it cleans everything up."

"You silly little boy," said the
old woman, and prodded me with
her bony finger. "It's my *flying*
broomstick. I ride it; only now I can't.
It doesn't work."

I thought she must be potty, but
anyway, I said, "You want to speak to
my brother Pete."

"Your brother Pete? Why should I speak to him?" she asked.

"Because he fixes things," I answered. "He's got a motor bike, and that keeps stopping, and he fixes it. He comes home this way; he'll be along in a minute."

"He can't fix his bike very well," said the old woman. "Not if it keeps stopping."

"It's a very old bike," I replied. "Pete says it's on its last legs."

"Mine's a very old broomstick." The old woman rubbed her chin. "Do you really think he could fix it?"

"Oh yes." I'd seen Pete fix his bike and our lawnmower, and even the vicar's old car which was falling to pieces.

I was certain he could fix a broomstick. I was also certain that broomsticks couldn't fly. That only happened in stories.

"You know what will happen if he says he can do it, and fails?" asked the old woman.

"He'll give you your money back," I replied. Pete had given the vicar his money back. He'd said that the vicar would do better to put it to a new car.

"If he fixes it," said the old woman, "I shall give him whatever he wants; his heart's desire. But if he fails ..." The old woman gave a high and horrible laugh. "If he fails I shall make him sleep for a hundred years."

"He'll like that," I told her. Apart from his motor bike, sleep was about the only thing that interested Pete.

"Well, I'll find something he *doesn't* like," said the old woman. "I'm a witch, you know, and quite a whiz of a witch. I'll think of something."

Just then we heard the sound of an engine, and a motor bike came round the bend in the road.

I jumped up and down, and waved. The bike pulled over and the rider lifted off his helmet. It was Pete; I could tell by his spots.

12

"Uh," he said. He didn't talk much, my brother.

"Pete," I said, "this old lady would like you to fix her broomstick."

"Uh?" said Pete.

"Young man," the witch said, "your little brother has told me that you can fix my flying broomstick. Can you?"

"Uh?" replied Pete.

"Pete!" I tugged at my brother's arm, and he bent down to hear me whisper. "She says she's a witch. I think she's off her trolley."

He started to get off his bike.

"And she says she'll do something terrible to you, if you fail," I added.

Pete put his bike on its stand, and went over to the broomstick. He picked it up and made a couple of sweeps with it, pushing some rubbish into a pile.

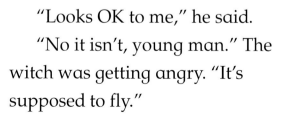

"Looks OK to me," he said.

"No it isn't, young man." The witch was getting angry. "It's supposed to fly."

"The broom will not go brrm-
brrm," I said, imitating the old
woman's voice.

She gave me a look which made
me wish I hadn't spoken, then turned
back to my brother and asked,
"Can you fix it?"

"OK," said Pete, and he fetched a
screwdriver from his bike.

"Pete!" I tugged at his arm. "Tell her you don't do broomsticks. Remember, she'll do something terrible to you if you say you can fix it when you can't." The old woman had frightened me, and while I still didn't really believe in witches, I thought it better not to take any chances.

"Don't worry, Squirt," replied Pete. "She can't harm us. I'll just do something to keep her happy, then we can go home for tea."

17

My brother fiddled about with the broom. He dug out lots of leaves and dirt from the brushes, then he stood up, winked at me and very seriously asked the old woman, "How d'you start it?"

"You bend the top of the stick to one side," replied the witch, "then you twist it."

Pete did as the witch had told him. Of course nothing happened, and Pete said with a frown, "I think you'll have to push it home or call out the breakdown truck."

I tried not to laugh, but couldn't stop myself and had to clap my hand over my mouth. Pete frowned at me, but I could see he was biting his lip to stop himself laughing.

"You told me you'd fix it!" she screeched. "You told me you'd fix it and you lied! I'm going to turn you into a frog. I shall turn you both into frogs!"

She seemed to grow, and I'm sure red sparks darted out of her eyes. She frightened me rigid, and even my brother must have been a bit scared because he twisted his hands nervously round the broomstick handle.

I was amazed at what happened next, but not half as amazed as Pete. His eyes were so wide I thought they would pop out. The broomstick coughed a couple of times, then stood there making a whirring noise.

"Try it round the block," Pete said to the witch.

"I'll do better than that," she said, and she sat astride the broomstick, and gave the top of the stick a big twist.

Broomstick and witch flew up into the air, and hovered just above the level of the rooftops. Then there was a huge BANG! Pete and I were covered in black soot.

The broomstick clattered into the
road, and the witch sailed down
slowly, with her skirts all puffed up
like a parachute.

"You young idiot!" shouted the
witch after she had reached the
ground and rolled over a couple
of times. "You nearly killed me!
I'm going to turn your bike into
a scooter."

23

"Not my fault," said Pete. "I said try it round the block, not over the moon!" and he went to work with his screwdriver again, fiddling about with the broomstick.

"There," he said at last. "Try it round the block. ROUND THE BLOCK!"

The witch got on to the broomstick again and twisted the handle.

Whoosh! She was gone; up the road and round the corner. And then *whoosh!* she was back, smiling all over her wrinkled old face.

"OK?" asked Pete.

"Brilliant!" replied the witch. "Good as new! I shall give you whatever you want. You shall have your heart's desire."

25

"It's OK," muttered Pete, and got
on his bike. "See you at home,
Squirt," he said to me, and off he
went on his old machine.

I looked round, but the witch
had gone. I could see her disappearing
over the church at the end of the road.
I went home.

The next morning, when I came downstairs, I saw a letter on the mat. It was addressed to Pete, so I took it up to him. I went into his room and jumped on him, on his bed, as I always do when I want to wake him up.

"Uh?" he said.

"You've got a letter!" I told him. "Here it is," and I gave it to him.

Pete opened the envelope and read the letter. Then suddenly he jumped out of bed, pulled on his jeans over his pyjamas, and rushed downstairs.

I picked up the letter and took it down to show my parents.

The letter said, "You shall have your heart's desire. It is outside."

My brother came bursting into the kitchen, crashing open the door and tripping over the dog's dinner bowl.

"Look at this!" he shouted. "Just come and look at this!" and he shot back out of the kitchen and out of the front door.

We all followed, and stood in the front doorway.

In the road was Pete's old bike, and behind that was Pete, standing by a brand spanking new motor bike. The very one he had always wanted. There it was. Not a dream, but there.

All gleaming and shiny.

"Wow!" I said.

"It looks terribly fast," said my
mother. "It looks as if it could *fly*."

"Well, aren't you going to try it?"
asked my father.

Pete sat astride the bike and started it. The engine purred sweetly, and Pete rode off round the block. He came back smiling all over his face.

"See if you can do a wheelie," I said.

"Why not?" said Pete. His old bike wouldn't pull the skin off a rice pudding, let alone pull a wheelie.

"Peter, I think you ought to ..."

"Really it would be better if ..."

My parents started speaking together, but Pete didn't hear them. He gave the grip on the handlebar a wrenching great twist. The bike reared up on its back wheel, and WHOOSH!! off it went, with Pete hanging on for dear life, not up the

road but up, up and away, over the
church roof and rising.

It was teatime before he came back. He was trembling all over. I could see his kneecaps bobbing up and down.

"What was it like, Pete?" I asked.

"Phew!" was all he said.

"Are you all right, dear?" asked my mother.

All Pete replied was "Phew!" But he never did say a lot, my brother.